SEVEN SCENES OF HALLOWEEN

Jeffrey M Jones

BROADWAY PLAY PUBLISHING INC
224 E 62nd St, NY, NY 10065
www.broadwayplaypub.com
info@broadwayplaypub.com

SEVENTY SCENES OF HALLOWEEN
© Copyright 1980 by Jeffrey M Jones

First printing, this edition: July 2005
This printing: February 2012
I S B N: 978-0-88145-273-0

Book design: Marie Donovan
Typeface: Palatino
Printed and bound in the U S A

This play is dedicated with love and gratitude to Joan Gregorius Jones

GENERAL NOTES

The play consists of interchangeable scenes arranged in a sequence. Different arrangements will create different "stories" with different "meanings".

All scenes take place in the living room of a rented house. There are entrances from the front hallway, the kitchen, and the upstairs. There is also a window with a view of the night outside, and a wall closet. The furnishings include two easy chairs and a television set. The television set remains on and audible throughout the entire play.

With a few exceptions, each scene begins as indicated with an audible cue to bring up the lights of the room. Usually this will be done by the stage manager, offstage. Each scene ends with a blackout taken on a silent, visual cue. That the television will partially illuminate the set-up between scenes is intentional.

There are four actors in the play, two men and two women, all in their early thirties. Both men wear an identical basic costume of everyday clothing, as do both women. These are the costumes of the characters JEFF and JOAN, usually played by ACTOR and ACTRESS 1.

There are also characters called GHOSTS. GHOSTS are created by draping an actor or actress with a common white bedsheet. Do *not* cut eyeholes in the sheet. It is usually not important which actor plays a GHOST, and at times it may be expedient to have the stage manager also become a GHOST.

The other two characters are masked characters, THE BEAST and THE WITCH, usually played by ACTOR and ACTRESS 2. These masks must be machine-made, store-bought Halloween masks. Generally speaking, the desirable ambiguity of these two more symbolic characters will be heightened by selecting more neutral, representational masks instead of grotesque or horrific masks. The rest of their costumes should be kept simple to facilitate quick changes, and should look homemade. It is not important that the underlying basic costume be totally concealed.

THE BEAST has an animal's head (stag?) and wears a bright nylon poncho with bright rubber kitchen gloves. THE WITCH has a woman's face (not necessarily old) and a black cape and gloves with the traditional conical hat.

The birdcall mentioned in the script should be of the variety that produces a chirping sound through the twisting of a metal pin in a wooden shank, rather than the kind you blow through. Such calls are available through the Audubon Society and L L Bean. The chicken is available at your local supermarket.

SEVENTY SCENES OF HALLOWEEN was originally produced by Creation Production Company at the Theatre at St. Clement's, New York City, September 18-October 12, 1980, with the following cast and creative contributors:

JEFF .... Christopher McCann
JOAN .... Frederikke Meister
BEAST .... Kevin O'Rourke
WITCH .... Carolyn McGee

Director .... Matthew Maguire
Design .... Jim Clayburgh
Costumes .... Maura Clifford

CHARACTERS

STAGE MANAGER
JEFF
JOAN
BEAST
WITCH
GHOSTS

THE FIRST SCENE

S.M.: *(Off)* Scene One—go!

(Lights up: ACTOR 1 *as* JEFF *is watching TV. He calls:)*

JEFF: Hey, Joan?

JOAN: *(Off)* What?

JEFF: Do we have any kandy korn?

JOAN: *(Off)* What?

JEFF: Do we have any kandy korn?

JOAN: *(Off)* What?

JEFF: Kandy korn!

Joan?...

JOAN: *(Off)* What?

JEFF: Can you hear me?

JOAN: *(Off)* I can't hear you!

JEFF: DO...WE...HAVE...ANY...KANDY KORN?

JOAN: *(Off)* Kandy korn?

JEFF: Yes!

JOAN: *(Off)* No!

JEFF: Well, why not, goddamn it?
I thought I told you to get some.
(Shit.)

JOAN: *(Off)* What?

JEFF: Never mind!

(ACTRESS 1 *as* JOAN *enters from kitchen.*)

JOAN: I can't hear a thing you're saying when I'm out
    there.
Not one word.

JEFF: I'm sorry.

JOAN: I just hate shouting across the house, I hate it.

JEFF: Sorry.

JOAN: Why, did you want some?

JEFF: It's not important.
Let's forget it.

JOAN: Fine.

(BLACKOUT)

THE SECOND SCENE

S.M.: *(Off)* Scene Two—go!

(Lights up: ACTRESS 1 *as* JOAN *is watching TV.* ACTOR 1
calls from offstage.)

JEFF: *(Off)* Hey, Joan?

JOAN: What?

JEFF: *(Off)* Do we have any kandy korn?

JOAN: In the kitchen.

JEFF: *(Off)* What?

JOAN: In the kitchen!

JEFF: *(Off)* I am in the kitchen!
Did you say it's in the kitchen?

JOAN: Yes!

JEFF: *(Off)* What? I can't hear you.

Joan?

JOAN: Yes!

JEFF: (*Off*) Did you say yes?

JOAN: Yes!

JEFF: (*Off*) Oh...okay....
I'm looking for it, but....

JOAN: Look in the cupboard over the sink.

JEFF: (*Off*) What?

JOAN: Look in the cupboard over the sink!

JEFF: (*Off*) I can't hear you!

JOAN: CUPBOARD...OVER...THE SINK!

JEFF: (*Off*) Wait a minute....

Never mind, I found it....
You know where it was?
It was in the cupboard over the sink.
I don't think that's such a great place for it, though.
Tell you what: I'm going to leave it in the pantry, okay?

Joan, is that okay?

JOAN: Yes!

JEFF: (*Off*) Okay.

(*The doorbell rings.*)

Will you get that?

(JOAN *is already going for the door.*)

Joan?

JOAN: Yes, I'm getting it!

(JOAN *exits toward front door.*)

(*BLACKOUT*)

THE THIRD SCENE

S.M.: *(Off)* Three—go!

(Lights up: ACTRESS 1 *as* JOAN *is watching TV. The doorbell rings.)*

JOAN: I'll get it.

JEFF: *(Off)* Will you get that?

JOAN: What?

JEFF: *(Off)* Will you get the door?

JOAN: *(Rising)* That's what I said.

JEFF: *(Off)* Sorry.

JOAN: That's all right.

(JOAN *exits toward the front door.* THE BEAST'*s head appears in the window.)*

(BLACKOUT)

THE FOURTH SCENE

S.M.: *(Off)* Four—go!

(THE BEAST'*s head is in the window; bare stage. From inside the closet comes the faint sound of scratching, then a birdcall.* ACTOR *&* ACTRESS 1 *call from offstage.)*

JEFF: *(Off)* Joan?

JOAN: *(Off)* I'm in the kitchen.

JEFF: *(Off)* Do we have any kandy korn?

JOAN: *(Off)* I'm in the kitchen.

JEFF: *(Off)* What?

JOAN: *(Off)* I can't hear you.

JEFF: *(Off)* Can you hear me?...

Joan?...

Hello?...

(ACTOR 1 *as* JEFF *enters from upstairs;* THE BEAST *disappears below window; the sounds stop.)*

Where are you?...

JOAN: *(Off)* Out in the kitchen.

JEFF: Oh, okay....

(JEFF *crosses the stage and exits toward kitchen.* THE BEAST *reappears and the sounds resume.)*

(BLACKOUT)

THE SIXTH SCENE

S.M.: *(Off)* Six—go!

(Lights up: ACTOR *&* ACTRESS 1 *as* JEFF *and* JOAN *are watching TV.)*

JEFF: Goddamn it!
Why the fuck didn't you get me that kandy korn like I
   asked?

JOAN: I'm sorry.
I didn't realize....

JEFF: Didn't I ask you?
Didn't I ask you specifically...?

JOAN: Yes!

I just didn't think it was that big a deal.

JEFF: Not that big a deal?
Jesus Christ!
I ask you specifically to get something and you say it's

not that big a deal?
I can't believe it—I fucking can't believe it!
It's like everything else!
It's like living with a fucking Mongolian idiot!

JOAN: Oh, shut up!
How was I supposed to know you wanted it for you?

JEFF: Well, who else...?

JOAN: I thought you just wanted me to get some for the
   kids!
All you said was: Get some kandy korn.
I thought you wanted it for the kids.

JEFF: So?

JOAN: So it's no good for the kids.
It's not wrapped.
If it's not wrapped they're not supposed to take it.
They even had a thing on the news.

JEFF: (Oh, Jesus!...)

Not you—I mean them. I'd forgotten about that.

JOAN: Besides, they didn't have any at the Pathmark
   store.

JEFF: Oh.

JOAN: If I'd known you'd wanted them I'd have looked
   elsewhere,
But you didn't make that clear.

JEFF: I know. I'm sorry.

JOAN: That's all right.

JEFF: You want to watch this program?

JOAN: It's fine.

(A GHOST *walks swiftly past the window, as:*
BLACKOUT.)

THE FIFTH SCENE

S.M.: *(Off)* Five—go!

(Lights up: ACTOR 1 *as* JEFF *is watching TV.*
ACTRESS 1 *as* JOAN *enters from kitchen with large knife.)*

JOAN: This knife is too dull, I can't cut with it.
I'm afraid to cut with it this way,
I'm afraid I'll cut myself, it's dangerous.
It's so dull, you know—it cuts,
But I'm afraid of it slipping and cutting my finger,
They do that sometimes when they get dull.

JEFF: Unh-hunh....

JOAN: So you'll sharpen it?

JEFF: What?

JOAN: You'll sharpen it?

JEFF: Yes.

Just leave it.

JOAN: You want me to leave it here?
Can I leave it here?
I'll leave it for you right here.
Is that okay?

JEFF: Fine.

JOAN: Okay.

I mean, I don't need it right away,
But as soon as you can get to it, that'll be great.
I mean, I could probably go ahead and use it anyway
    but I'm afraid to cut myself,
You know?

JEFF: Right.

JOAN: Is there a better place to leave it?

JEFF: I'm watching TV.

JOAN: Oh.
Sorry.

(BLACKOUT)

THE THIRTY-FIFTH SCENE

S.M.: *(Off)* Thirty-five—go!

(Lights up: ACTOR *&* ACTRESS 1 *as* JEFF *&* JOAN *are watching TV.* ACTOR 2 *as* THE BEAST *looks in from the window, working the birdcall.* JEFF *&* JOAN *do not react as they chant:)*

BEAST: Sometimes when I look up...

JEFF & JOAN: ...in the bare branches

BEAST: I notice the bird...

JEFF & JOAN: ...fly up in the branches

BEAST: I notice the branches...

JEFF & JOAN: ...in the bare branches

BEAST: I feel the bird call me...

JEFF & JOAN: ...out of the branches

BEAST: I feel the bird's eye on me...

JEFF & JOAN: ...up in the branches

BEAST: I feel the cold wind...

JEFF & JOAN: ...blow through the bare branches

BEAST: I feel very hungry...

JEFF & JOAN: ...looking up at the branches

BEAST: I shout up my shout...

JEFF & JOAN: ...back into the branches

BEAST: Then I notice the bird fall...

JEFF & JOAN: ...out of the branches

BEAST: Then I feel afraid of the bird
Then I become the bird

JEFF & JOAN: Then I feel afraid of the bird
Then I become the bird

BEAST: Then I am standing alone again underneath
  the bare branches

JEFF & JOAN: And the leaves are falling down all 'round
  me
From the bare branches....

ALL: OHHHHHHHHHHHHHHI IHHHH!

I...AM...SO...HUNGRYYYYYYYY!

YAH!

(A GHOST *pops out of the closet and runs briefly about the
room, fluttering and peeping.)*

GHOST: Feeeeeeeeed meeeeeeeee......
Feeeeeeeeed meeeeeeeee......
Feeeeeeeeed meeeeeeeee......

(BLACKOUT)

THE SEVENTH SCENE

S.M.: *(Off)* Seven—go!

(Lights up: ACTOR *&* ACTRESS 1 *as* JEFF *&* JOAN *are
watching TV. Beat.)*

JEFF: Scared of me?

JOAN: Well, kind of....
But it's not *you*: I just....
I just want to curl up and hide, that's all.
I don't know.

JEFF: Well, shit—I'm no ball of fire myself,
  sometimes—you know?
I mean, I get scared too, I guess.
I get squeamish—I guess that's the same thing....

It's like I'm profoundly ambivalent:
Either it's Fantasyland, right? You know?
Turn-on City, swinging from the chandeliers (I mean, in
  my mind);
Or else it's still something that's somehow degrading
  and...
You know, that kind of thing.
And I feel: If I could just find a middle ground....

I mean, your feelings are: It's either this or that—
And you have to stop and say to yourself: Now wait, I
  know it's not *really* like that;
Even so, that doesn't automatically change the way you
  feel.
Does this make sense?

JOAN: Unh-hunh.

JEFF: Like that's why I say sometimes, you know:
Don't necessarily believe me when I act uninterested.
I mean, sometimes I have to be convinced.
Like a lot of times, I start out thinking I'm really turned
  off,
And then once I get into it I go: Hey, this is really *great*!
So that's what I mean when I say sometimes I have to
  look to you to start things.

JOAN: Yeah, but see: When you're not interested it's
  hard for me to keep going because I don't know, and
  sometimes I...
I mean, I don't want to get all excited and then have no
  place to go, you know?

(*The doorbell rings.*)

JEFF: (I'll get it in a sec:) Right.

JOAN: I guess it goes back to living with Lance:
I mean, he used to get me so turned on,
We'd be making out for hours, literally, with no clothes
    on;
I would try everything, but he just wouldn't fuck me.
I got so frustrated....
I mean, that's where I learned to shut down.

(The doorbell rings.)

That's also why, man, when you lose it, that's it for me.
I don't want to have to go digging around for it.
I'm not begging for it.

JEFF: I gotta get the door—don't forget where we are, I'll
    be right back.

(JEFF *exits toward front door.*)

(BLACKOUT)

THE EIGHTH SCENE

S.M.: *(Off)* Eight—go!

(Lights up: ACTRESS 1 *as* JOAN *is watching TV.* ACTOR 1 *as*
JEFF *enters from front door.)*

JOAN: Well?

JEFF: Just as I suspected, Roderigo:
Another visit from the tiny humanoids.

JOAN: Ahah!

JEFF: Yes, it's true: miniature people.
Midgets, perhaps, or dwarves.
It was hard to tell what they were underneath their
    sinister disguises.

JOAN: Really?
But, Jeff—what do they want with us?

JEFF: Food, Joan!
Ritual offerings.
Actually, they were extremely direct:
Either I supplied them *tout-de-suite avec* le grub, or
else....

JOAN: Yes?

JEFF: There were threats, Joan, let's just say there were
    threats.

JOAN: I see.

JEFF: Yes.

JOAN: Sounds pretty serious.

JEFF: It was hell.

JOAN: So what happened?

JEFF: Joan—what could I do—I'm a man—I was weak.
Quickly assessing their depraved little needs,
I proceeded to offer them large amounts of sugary
    substances.
Of course, I knew they had too much already:
Their hands, their mouths were sticky with the stuff!
But I was reckless—I gave them more, more, *all they
    wanted*!
And then, suddenly, as quickly as they had come,
They disappeared into the darkness that spawned them.
And tonight, this living nightmare is endlessly
    replaying itself
In every small suburban town
Somewhere, in the Twilight Zone (Dee-dee dee-dee,
    dee-dee dee-dee....)

So, what are you watching? Hunh, baby?

(JOAN *shakes her head: She doesn't know. They both start to
laugh.*)

No?

JOAN: Don't ask me, boy—you know....
I don't know....

JEFF: Nothing, hunh?
Nichts? Not one thing?

JOAN: Nope.

JEFF: I'll bet you don't even know the name of it, do you?
Hunh? Come on, now....

JOAN: I do so—it's *(name of actual program)*.

JEFF: Here, let me get you another drink.

(JEFF *exits toward kitchen with glasses.*)

JOAN: Sure, baby!
I say—let the party begin!

(BLACKOUT)

THE NINTH SCENE

S.M.: *(Off)* Nine—go!

(*Lights up:* ACTRESS 1 *as* JOAN *is watching TV.*)

JOAN: No—I don't want them either.
Not right now, at any rate—I'm not ready.
I've really made up my mind about that—I mean, for right now.

I was talking to Laura, you know, about this?
(She's so great!)
Anyway, I really realized—I was so *rooked* as a kid—
I mean, forget it, I was never allowed to be a kid.
I had to be this perfect little grown-up, you know?

ACTOR 1: *(Off)* Meanwhile your parents are acting like children, right?

JOAN: Yeah—so now that I'm grown up,
Now that I've got a house of my own, boy—
I'm gonna be the baby for a while.
I'm basically very selfish, I'm very needy.
I don't need some other human being feeding off of me.
I don't need to get it from both sides.
I just want to be left alone to play.

(The doorbell rings.)

ACTOR 1: *(Off)* Go away! Go away! There's nobody
  home and we eat little children!

JOAN: That's okay, I'll get it.

(JOAN *rises and exits toward front door.*
Beat.
ACTRESS 2 *calls feebly from inside closet.)*

ACTRESS 2: *(Off)* Come back...let me out....
Help...let me out....

Joooaaaaaaaaaaannnnn....

(BLACKOUT)

THE TENTH SCENE

S.M.: *(Off)* Ten—go!

(Lights up: ACTRESS 2, *as* WITCH, *unmasked, stands down
center. Another* WITCH, *masked, watches TV throughout
scene.)*

ACTRESS 2: "We had lost our way.
The forest grew darker,
And together we walked hand-in-hand until we came
  upon a cottage in a clearing.
We knocked on the door; nobody answered.
We peered through the windows; nothing was there.
And so, at last, we lay down together and cried
  ourselves to sleep.

In the middle of the night, I heard a voice sweetly
  calling my name.
I saw the inside of the cottage ablaze with light.
I turned back to where we were sleeping, but no one
  was there.
And when I looked through the door I saw a table piled
  with food and one chair and one plate and one knife.
It seemed however much I ate, I was never full;
And whenever I looked away, there was more on my
  plate.
At last, a great drowsiness overwhelmed me and I
  climbed the stair to the four-poster bed,
Falling into a slumber on a great white counterpane.

But when I awoke for the second time, it was in
  darkness.
I was locked in a room so small I could hardly stand.
I cried for help for hours but nobody came.
And then I knew that I should never see my home
  again,
And that I had been utterly transformed."

(ACTOR 2 *calls from inside closet, pounding on door:*)

ACTOR 2: Let...me...out!...

(*BLACKOUT*)

THE ELEVENTH SCENE

S.M.: (*Off*) Eleven—go!

(*Lights up:* ACTRESS 1 *as* JOAN *is watching TV.*
ACTOR 1 *as* JEFF *enters from front door.*)

JEFF: ...Pathetic, boy—absolutely *pa*-thetic (piss me off....)

JOAN: What?

JEFF: Oh, this kid that was just out there:
He had all these weird pieces of cardboard stuck on his

body.
So I asked him, I said: What are you supposed to be?
Kid says: I don't know.
So I said: You mean to tell me you make your own
    costume and you don't even know who you're
    supposed to be?
Kid goes: Can I just have my candy now, Mister?
Jesus (Unbelievable!) I almost didn't give it to him.
And his sister had some dumb Da-Glo painted sheet
    on—
I mean these are not costumes!

JOAN: Who were they?

JEFF: Oh, just some—I don't know—kids that live in
    that house down the—you know.
I've seen them playing on the—you've seen 'em.
If you'd seen them you'd know.
The ones that are always out there?
Kid with the glasses, you know, looks about 45 and
    vicious?

JOAN: Unh-hunh....

JEFF: You know the ones I mean?

JOAN: Not really.

JEFF: Ah—forget it, it's not important.

I HATE KIDS!
God! Let's never have any!
All they do is smell funny and scream and yell and fight
    and eat and get into trouble and get hurt and
    make you spend all your money.
One of Nature's less-good ideas.

JOAN: Well, I can see my sweetie's in a good mood.

JEFF: I'm kidded out, Joan; I'm suffering from
    Kiddy-Overload.
You ever tried to have a conversation with an

eight-year-old?
"Hello, children: I'm your adult neighbor, and I'm only
   slightly lame...."

I mean, they're worse than grown-ups!
At least with grown-ups you don't have to be nice.

JOAN: *(Rising)* You want another drink? I'll make you
   one.

JEFF: Please! And make it strong!

(JOAN exits toward kitchen. The doorbell rings.)

WE'RE NOT HOME!

JOAN: *(Off)* I'll get it!

JEFF: You just make the drinks!
I'll get it! (Little fuckers!)

(JEFF exits toward front door.)

(BLACKOUT)

THE TWELFTH SCENE

S.M.: *(Off)* Twelve—go!

*(Lights up: Bare stage.
The closet door is shut and from inside comes loud pounding.
ACTOR 2 is heard bellowing from inside closet:)*

ACTOR 2: *(Off)* FEEEEEEEED MEEEEEEEEEE...

FEEEEEEEEEEEEEEEEED
MEEEEEEEEEEEEEEEEEEE...

I...AM...SO...HUN...GRY....

AHHHHHHHHHHHHHHHHHHHHHHHHHH!

IIIIII...AMMMMM...SOOOOO...HUNNNN...GRYYYYY!

(Furious pounding. BLACKOUT)

THE SEVENTEENTH SCENE

S.M.: *(Off)* Seventeen—go!

(Lights up: ACTOR 1 *as* JEFF *is watching TV.*
He lights a joint; the doorbell rings.)

JEFF: *(Calls)* Will you get that?

*(*ACTRESS 1 *answers from offstage.)*

ACTRESS 1: *(Off)* In a minute.

JEFF: *(Calls)* Okay.

(Beat.
The doorbell rings again.)

Joan?

ACTRESS 1: *(Off)* I'm coming, I'm coming....

*(*ACTRESS 1 *as* JOAN *enters from upstairs.)*

JEFF: And listen—don't let them in, don't let them smell
   it, okay?
Like, just open the door a crack.
Or am I being paranoid?

Can you smell it?

JOAN: Of course.

JEFF: Yeah, but could you like, smell it upstairs?

JOAN: Of course.

JEFF: Shit, what if it's the cops?

JOAN: It's not the cops.
It's Tommy and Little Artie, I saw them out the
   bedroom.

JEFF: Oh.

JOAN: I'll handle it.

(JOAN *exits toward front door.*)

JEFF: *(Calls)* Or listen, you could just deal with them out
  on the porch, that would work.
Don't you think?
Or do you?
Maybe it's—or do whatever you want. I'm watching TV.

(BLACKOUT)

THE EIGHTEENTH SCENE

S.M.: *(Off)* Eighteen—go!

(Lights up: ACTOR & ACTRESS 1 *as* JEFF & JOAN *are
watching TV.* JOAN *rises.*)

JEFF: Will you make me one?

JOAN: I wasn't going into the kitchen.

JEFF: Oh. Sorry....

JOAN: Why? Do you need another one?

JEFF: No, no, I'm fine, actually....

(JOAN exits upstairs; JEFF *keeps watching TV.*)

Oh, wow—look at that! *(Calls)* Joan! Quick! Come look
  at this!
Hurry, hurry, hurry!
Oh, wait...never mind....

(JOAN enters from upstairs.)

JOAN: What is it?

JEFF: That's all right—never mind—I'm sorry....
There was this thing on TV I wanted you to see it, but...
It's gone.

JOAN: Oh. Okay.

(JOAN exits upstairs; JEFF *keeps watching TV. Beat.*)

JEFF: *(Calls)* It's back!...Quick! Joan?
If you want to see it, hurry!

(JOAN enters from stairs.)

JOAN: *What?*

JEFF: No—shit—you just missed it.
Don't worry—it'll come right back.
Wait a minute—I'm sure they'll cut right back to it now.

JOAN: What is it?

JEFF: Hang on a sec, you'll see....
(Oh, this is really boring right now....)
It's this, this—you'll see, you'll see....
(Oh, come on!...?) I can't believe they're not showing it.

JOAN: Well, look, if they do, you can let me know.

(JOAN exits upstairs.)

JEFF: Yeah, I'll holler. Sorry to drag you away....
Once you see it, you'll see though:
I mean, it's not all that big a deal, but it's still kind of far
    out, you know what I mean?...
Joan?... Can you hear me?... Hey, Joan?...

JOAN: *(Off)* Is it on?

JEFF: No, no, that's all right—it's not on yet! Don't come!

(JOAN enters from upstairs.)

I'm sorry—it was a mistake—it's not on....

JOAN: Well, I thought you were calling me.

JEFF: I know, I know—I tried to explain, I guess you
    couldn't hear:
See, I was afraid where you were, you wouldn't be able
    to hear me.
So then I called to see if you could hear me,
And then I realized...oh, never mind....
Next time I'll only call if it's on, okay?

JOAN: Look—I'm trying to start getting ready—just tell
  me what it is so I don't have to keep running down
  here all the time.

JEFF: Forget it—it's not that big a deal.
Definitely not worth running up and down for....
It's nothing—
I mean, I'd try and explain it in words but you'd
  think it was nothing.
(It *is* nothing.)
I mean, if you saw it, you'd kind of get off on it, but....
No, it's definitely not worth running up and down for.

JOAN: So, now—what?
Are you calling me or what?

JEFF: No, not unless you want me to.
But if you want me to I will.
(Except how would you know?)

JOAN: Exactly.

JEFF: So then I won't, okay?

JOAN: Fine.

JEFF: Good.
Believe me, it was nothing that big....

(JOAN *exits upstairs.*)

Sorry....

JOAN: *(Off)* It's all right.

(Beat)

JEFF: It's back, if you're interested.
You're probably not interested, though, at this point.
Never mind!

(JOAN *enters from upstairs.*)

It was just back but you're probably not interested,
  hunh?

JOAN: Can we just forget about it, do you mind?

JEFF: Hunh?—Oh, sure, no, yeah, I'm sorry.
I'm sorry, sweetie.

(The doorbell rings.)

Do you mind?...
Or, no, no, that's all right—you sit, I'll get it.
You've been running up and down, you sit.
Just, if you can, kind of keep track of what's going on,
   okay?
Are you okay?
You're not mad at me, are you?

(The doorbell rings again.)

Wait a minute—I'll be right back and we can talk about
   it.
Just kind of try and keep track of the story, okay?

*(*JEFF *exits toward front door.*
The doorbell rings again.)

(Off) I'm coming!...

(BLACKOUT)

THE NINETEENTH SCENE

S.M.: *(Off)* Nineteen—go!

(Lights up: ACTOR *&* ACTRESS 1 *as* JEFF *&* JOAN *are
watching TV. The doorbell rings.)*

JEFF: Do you mind, or....

JOAN: What?

JEFF: Getting the door....

JOAN: No, not really, I guess.

JEFF: Or do you want me to?
I mean, I will...if you want....

JOAN: No, that's all right.

(JOAN *rises.*)

JEFF: See, it's just—
I've been doing it all night and I'm kind of getting tired
   of jumping up and down all the time and never
   getting a chance to relax for a minute.

JOAN: I know.

JEFF: You don't want to have to do it either, right?

JOAN: It's not that big a deal.

JEFF: Yeah, but still—you'd really rather not, right?

JOAN: I don't mind....

(JOAN *exits toward front door.*)

JEFF: (You're fucking lying to me, Joan....)

(*BLACKOUT*)

THE TWENTIETH SCENE

S.M.: (*Off*) Twenty—go!

(*Lights up:* ACTOR *&* ACTRESS 1 *as* JEFF *&* JOAN *are
watching TV. The doorbell rings.*)

JEFF: You want me to get it?

JOAN: No, that's all right.

JEFF: No, you want me to get it, don't you?

JOAN: Except that you don't want to.
I know that. It's fine.

JEFF: That's not what I'm asking you, Joan.
I'm asking if you want me to go get it, and you
   do—right?
And now you're all mad at me—right?
I mean, why do you have to be so passive?

Why can't you just say what you want?
Sure, I don't particularly like getting the door, but I will;
I'd do anything to avoid all this passive-aggressive
  bullshit!

JOAN: Oh, fuck you! Jesus!

(JOAN *storms out toward the front door.*)

JEFF: *(Calls)* Well, now what?
Are you getting the door or what?

(Beat)

(BLACKOUT)

THE TWENTY-FIRST SCENE

S.M.: *(Off)* Twenty-one—go!

(Lights up: ACTOR & ACTRESS 1 *as* JEFF & JOAN *are*
watching TV. The doorbell rings.)

JEFF: ...I'll get it....

JOAN: Never mind—I'll get it in a minute.

JEFF: I said, I'll get it, Joan.

JOAN: God, can't you just let me sit here a minute
  without badgering me?!

JEFF: But that's just it, that's just it!
I mean, you say you're going to get the door and then
  all you do is just sit around!
It's driving me crazy!
If you want me to get it, say so—say so!
Why do we have to go through all this weird
  manipulation shit?

JOAN: Oh, don't give me that shit!
You're the one who's manipulating!
You just want me to take care of it!

JEFF: And you don't want to, do you?
That's all I'm trying to get you to admit.
And then you get all defensive and hostile!
God, I don't know why you keep doing it!

JOAN: Because you're the one who's so fucking hostile
   all the time, and I just keep hoping if I get the
   goddamned door and leave you alone, maybe
   you'll simmer down!

JEFF: Then get it! Go get it!
Why the fuck don't you get it instead of sitting around?
I can't stand it!

(JEFF *storms out upstairs.*
The doorbell rings again.)

(*BLACKOUT*)

THE TWENTY-SECOND SCENE

ACTRESS 1: (*Softly*) Twenty-two—go!

(*Lights up:* ACTRESS 1 *as* JOAN *is watching TV. Beat.*
ACTOR 1 *as* JEFF *appears from closet, screaming in rage.*)

JEFF: All right! I fucked her!
Is that what you want to hear?
Is it?
You wanted to know, goddamn it, you're going to
   know:
Three times I fucked her!
One right after the other (which we *never* do)
And the third time in the morning!
And I can get hard right now just thinking about it.
And, yes—I feel guilty—okay?
And, yes—I know it's fucking everything up—okay?
And I'm not saying it's right or it's wrong except it's
   something I've wanted all my life and now I have

the chance for it and I am not going to spend the rest
of my life wishing I hadn't let it slip away!

Does this mean anything to you or are you too fucked
up with your own self-pity?
I mean, look at you—look at you!
Nine years!
Nine fucking years, Joan, and none of it matters,
does it?
We might just as well be goddamn assholes like
everybody else, you know?
I mean, I really thought, I really thought I could be
honest with you and you'd understand—not like it,
but at least understand—because it was just my trip,
it had to do with something I needed....
It has nothing to do with you! Nothing!
But I was wrong, wasn't I? I was a fool!
I should have lied to you!
I never should have told you anything at all,
and it would have been over
and you never would have known.
I was a fucking idiot, wasn't I?
Oh, for Christ's sake, can't you say an-y-thing?
An-y-thinggggggg, Joan? HUNH?
Oh, Jesus, I hate it when you're like this.
Say something!
Say something!

JOAN: *(Softly)* I love you....

JEFF: You love me...bullshit!
Because your love is like a jail!

(JEFF *storms out toward kitchen. Beat.)*

JOAN: *(Softly)* Blackout.

(BLACKOUT)

THE FIFTEENTH SCENE

S.M.: *(Off)* Fifteen—go!

(Lights up: ACTOR *&* ACTRESS 1 *as* JEFF *&* JOAN *are watching TV.*
A GHOST *is seen just disappearing at the window.*
The doorbell rings.)

JEFF: I'll get it.

(No movement. Beat.
JEFF *rises and exits toward front door.*
The closet door slowly opens and ACTRESS 2 *calls from within.)*

ACTRESS 2: *(Off)* Joooaaannn....

Joooooaaaaannnnn....

*(*JOAN *rises stiffly, turns, walks toward closet, exiting.)*

J o o o o a a a a a n n n n n . . . .

*(*ACTRESS 2 *cackles from closet.)*

(BLACKOUT)

THE TWENTY-THIRD SCENE

S.M.: *(Off)* Twenty-three—go!

(Lights up: Bare stage.
Knocking from inside closet, and ACTRESS 2 *calls from offstage:)*

ACTRESS 2: *(Off)* Help!
Let me out!
Let me out of here!
Someone!
Anyone! Help!

If you can hear me, let me out of here! Please!
I'll give you anything! Anything!
Is there anybody out there?
Hello?
Hello?

(THE BEAST *enters with a kitchen knife raised, approaches* closet.)

Who is that?

What are you doing?

No!
Noooooo!
Please, no, don't do it, pleeeeeeeease....

(THE BEAST *sticks the knife into the closet door.*
ACTRESS 2 *screams horribly.*
THE BEAST *turns and exits.*)

(BLACKOUT)

THE TWENTY-FOURTH SCENE

S.M.: *(Off)* Twenty-four—go!

(Lights up: ACTOR 1, *as* JEFF, *masked as* BEAST, *and*
ACTRESS 1, *as* JOAN, *masked as* WITCH, *are watching TV.*
ACTOR 2, *as* BEAST, *unmasked, and* ACTRESS 2, *as* WITCH,
unmasked, call from outside window:)

ACTOR & ACTRESS 2: Hi! Hi!
Hi, you guys! Hi!
Hi, Jeff! Hi, Joan!
How you doin'?
Hey, Happy Halloween, you guys!
Hey, it's us, guys.
Hey, open up!
Jeff? Joan?
(Maybe they can't hear us.)

Hey—hello in there!
Hello?
Hey, come on, let us in.
Hey, quit fooling around.
Hey, it's Halloween!
(They must be ignoring us.)
Trick or treat!
Hey, come on, it's getting cold out here!
(Go see if the front door's open....)
Hey, we're coming around to the front.

(ACTOR & ACTRESS 2 *disappear.*)

(*The doorbell rings.*)

(*The doorbell rings.*)

(*The doorbell rings.*)

(JEFF & JOAN *still do not react.*)

(*BLACKOUT*)

THE TWENTY-FIFTH SCENE

S.M.: (*Off*) Twenty-five—go!

(*Lights up:* ACTRESS 1, *as* JOAN, *masked as* WITCH, *and* ACTOR 1, *as* JEFF, *masked as* BEAST, *are watching TV. Allow a beat.*)

JOAN: It's betting kind of moist in here....

Getting all sticky...

JEFF: Damp....
Very damp....
Very soggy....

(*Suddenly and for no apparent reason,* JEFF *yells. Beat.* JOAN *turns to him.*)

JOAN: Now what?

JEFF: I keep bumping my eyelashes, it's very
    uncomfortable,
My eyelashes, I keep bumping them against something,
I think it's the edge of the eyehole or something,
It's driving me crazy.

(Beat.
JEFF *then pushes the mask around on his face as*
ACTRESS 2 *shrieks from the closet.)*

There....
That's better....

JOAN: *(Beat. Pointing at TV)* Who is that actor?

(BLACKOUT)

THE TWENTY-SEVENTH SCENE (A + B)

S.M.: *(Off)* Twenty-seven A—go!

(Lights up: ACTOR & ACTRESS 1 *as* JEFF & JOAN *are
watching TV.*
ACTOR & ACTRESS 2 *as* BEAST & WITCH *are outside
window, tapping on the pane, calling "Trick or Treat!", etc.,
while* JEFF & JOAN *studiously ignore them.)*

JEFF: *(Out of the corner of his mouth, sotto voce)* Pretend
    they're not there....

JOAN: *(Ditto)* I am...

JEFF: *(Ditto)* Driving me crazy....

JOAN: *(As before)* Me too....

(The doorbell starts ringing.
Pictures start rattling on the walls.
It gets noisier and noisier.
*Perhaps the remarks become more personal and somewhat
    obscene....*

Suddenly JEFF *leaps out of his chair and runs toward the front door, yelling:)*

JEFF: I am going to KILL THOSE MOTHERFUCKERS!!!!!!!!

(And everything disappears as if on cue.)

JOAN: They're gone.

JEFF: What happened?

(BLACKOUT)

S.M.: *(Off)* ...and B—go!

(Lights up: JEFF *has crossed to TV to change channels.* JOAN *is looking out the window.)*

JOAN: You really think they're gone?

(Unobserved, part of a GHOST's *sheet flutters from closet.)*

JEFF: Sure....

(BLACKOUT)

THE FOURTEENTH SCENE

S.M.: *(Off)* Fourteen—go!

(Lights up: ACTOR *&* ACTRESS 1 *as* JEFF *&* JOAN *are watching TV.)*

JEFF: Can you imagine what it must be like being eaten by an animal?
I was just thinking about that....

I mean, not just the pain (which I'm sure is intense)
But the horror....

*(*JOAN *rises.)*

JOAN: Yeah?...Go ahead, keep talking....

*(*JOAN *crosses to closet, opens door, and exits within.)*

JEFF: It's like, I was watching this program, this nature
    program,
And it suddenly hit me:
All it was was animals eating each other.
They had bugs jumping on other bugs, biting into them
    with their pincers (and then they always show the
    juice running out);
It was great, they had everything: birds and bugs, frogs
    and bugs;
Lots of bugs. (Bugs get eaten.)
But then—they had this whole sequence where this
    pack of hyenas surrounded a baby water-buffalo or
    something,
And they were running around,
And the mother was trying to chase them away,
And finally one of them just grabs it right by the throat
    and pulls it down on the ground and then they were
    all over it,
They showed one of them running away with the
    whole hind leg ripped off and bleeding in its mouth...

I mean, *strong* stuff!
But like, the way they present it, it's like they don't even
    know what they're looking at.
It's like weird propaganda, you know?
With the bouncy little soundtrack and the dippy
    announcer going: "And so, life goes on on the
    Serengeti...."
And I mean, this is for children?
This is so they won't have their minds warped by
    sex-and-violins?
Good, wholesome family entertainment, right?
You know what I mean?

Joan?

(ACTRESS 2 *as* JOAN *walks very quickly from closet to
kitchen.*)

ACTRESS 2: Right.

JEFF: ...Joanie???...

(No sooner does ACTRESS 2 *as* JOAN *exit by kitchen than* ACTRESS 1 *as* JOAN *enters from kitchen—as if she'd just turned around.)*

JOAN: I heard you—what is it?

JEFF: ...Nothing.... Forget it....

(BLACKOUT)

THE SIXTEENTH SCENE

S.M.: *(Off)* Sixteen—go!

(Lights up: ACTOR 1 *as* JEFF *is watching TV,* ACTRESS 1 *as* JOAN *leans against wall by kitchen entrance.)*

JOAN: We've got ants.

JEFF: Hunh?

JOAN: Ants.

JEFF: Isn't that just what you said?

JOAN: Yeah—we've got ants, they're everywhere.
All in the sugar and honey and everywhere.

JEFF: Really?

JOAN: I had to throw them all out.

JEFF: Really? That's so weird.
I mean, isn't it too late for ants, I mean too cold outside?
I thought they hibernated or something. (Maybe not.)
Hunh.

JOAN: What's even weirder is they were all inside of jars
  that had tops on them too, just solid ants crawling
  around on top of each other, just these bottles full of
  insects....

JEFF: (Gross.)

JOAN: ...It was gross, I threw them out.
I also had to throw out the flour, there were bugs in it,
    these little black things, these little black specks....

JEFF: You sure it wasn't pepper or something?

JOAN: There were wings.
I sifted some to see.
There was also this big white soft fat thing that was...

JEFF: Please! What a gross-out!

JOAN: It was laying eggs, I think.
So then I went to the refrigerator, you know? (Just
    checking.)

JEFF: Unh-hunh....

JOAN: Well, first of all, there were maggots.
Maggots in the cheese, maggots in the milk, maggots in
    the eggs, threw them all out.
Then, in the lettuce, those little centipede things with
    the jaws? Threw all that out too.
Oh—by the way—there's a whole calf's head in the
    freezer but the neck part got stuck to the metal so I
    thought I'd let you take care of that.
Besides, the closet is full of snakes.
You don't believe me, do you?
You think I'm making it all up.
Listen—can't you hear them slithering around in there?
You don't believe me? They're this high in there.
You want me to show you?
Come here—open it yourself.
You open the door and they'll all come tumbling out all
    over you.
In fact, when you open the door, be sure you stand off
    to one side out of the way.
In fact, don't!
Don't open the door. Okay?
Don't open it.

We'll just keep it shut, I'll get the snake man in the
  morning.

(JOAN *exits swiftly toward kitchen.*)

(BLACKOUT)

THE TWENTY-EIGHTH SCENE

S.M.: *(Off)* Twenty-eight—go!

*(Lights up: Bare stage. The closet door is ajar; birdcall sounds.
A* GHOST *enters tentatively from closet, crossing toward
  kitchen.
Abruptly,* ACTOR 1 *calls from offstage.)*

ACTOR 1: *(Off)* Joan?...
Where are you?...

(THE GHOST *immediately runs back into closet.)*

Joan?...

(Several other GHOSTS *run from kitchen into closet.*
ACTOR 1 *as* JEFF *enters from kitchen with shoebox.)*

Joanieeeeeeeeeeeeeee?...

(JEFF *crosses and exits upstairs.)*

ACTRESS 1: *(Off)* What?

ACTOR 1: *(Off)* Where the hell are you?

ACTRESS 1: *(Off)* In here.

ACTOR 1: *(Off)* Where the hell is here?

ACTRESS 1: *(Off)* What?

ACTOR 1: *(Off)* Where are you?

(ACTRESS 1 *as* JOAN *enters stealthily from closet, shutting
  door.
She crosses to chair quickly and sits, watching TV.)*

JOAN: Right here!
I'm watching television.

What do you need?

ACTOR 1: *(Off)* Nothing.
Forget it.

(BLACKOUT)

THE THIRTEENTH SCENE

S.M.: *(Off)* Thirteen—go!

(Lights up: ACTRESS 1 *as* JOAN *is watching TV.*
ACTOR 1 *as* JEFF *enters from front door with shoebox.)*

JEFF: Look what I found.

JOAN: What?

JEFF: This was just sitting on the front porch.
Somebody must have left it....(I guess.)

JOAN: Just like that?
Weird.
What's inside?

JEFF: I don't know.
You want to open it?

JOAN: Not really.

*(*JEFF *weighs box in his hand.)*

JEFF: Not real heavy....

*(*JEFF *shakes box.)*

Doesn't rattle....
Okay, here we go now....

*(*JEFF *opens box.)*

Hunh!

JOAN: What is it?

JEFF: Nothing. There's nothing in here.

JOAN: That's bizarre.

JEFF: Yeah, it's either that or it's very dull, I'll tell you.

(The doorbell rings.)

I'll get it.

(JEFF *leaves box behind, exits toward front door.*
As JOAN *watches TV, the birdcall sounds.*
Abruptly, she stands up and calls:)

JOAN: I'll put it in the closet!

(BLACKOUT)

THE THIRTY-FIRST SCENE

S.M.: *(Off)* Thirty-one—go!

(Lights up: ACTRESS 1 *as* JOAN *is watching TV.*
ACTOR 1 *as* JEFF *enters from front door with shoebox.)*

JEFF: Look at this.

JOAN: What?

JEFF: Found this box out on the porch like,
Somebody left it out there or something.

JOAN: You mean kids?

JEFF: May-be.
It was really—it was placed, you know, right in the
   middle.
Something about the way it was positioned.

JOAN: That's weird.

JEFF: Yeah.

(JEFF *rattles box.)*

JOAN: What is it?

JEFF: There's something inside here.

JOAN: I know, but what?

JEFF: How would I know?

(JEFF *opens box; inside is the* BEAST *mask.*)

That's it.
That's all there is.

JOAN: Here, let me see it.
Let me see the box, too.

(JOAN *tries on the mask.*)

How do I look?

JEFF: Hunh?

JOAN: How do I look?

JEFF: No, I'm fine.

JOAN: What?

JEFF: I'll get it.

(*The doorbell rings.* JEFF *crosses to stairs, climbs and exits.*)

JOAN: Do you want me to?

JEFF: No, that's okay.

JOAN: Are you sure?

JEFF: (*Off*) No, it's fine, really.

(*A* GHOST *appears in each entrance; birdcall sounds.*
JOAN, *masked, rises with box and exits through closet,*
GHOSTS *following.*)

(*BLACKOUT*)

THE THIRTIETH SCENE

S.M.: *(Off)* Thirty—go!

(Lights up: Bare stage.
ACTOR 1 *as* JEFF *enters from front door with shoebox.*
He calls:)

JEFF: Hey, Joan?
Joanie?
Look what I found.

ACTRESS 1: *(Off)* What did you say?

JEFF: I found something.

ACTRESS 1: *(Off)* What?

*(*JEFF *shakes box, opens it, finds a birdcall.)*

JEFF: Weird: it's a box with a—looks like a birdcall or
  something in it....

*(*JEFF *works the birdcall.)*

That's what it is, all right.

ACTRESS 1: *(Off)* Are you talking to me?

(The doorbell rings.)

JEFF: I'll get it.

ACTRESS 1: *(Off)* Will you get that?

JEFF: That's what I said.

*(*JEFF *exits toward front door.*
A GHOST *enters from closet, removes box and birdcall, and*
returns to closet, closing the door again.)

(BLACKOUT)

THE THIRTY-SECOND SCENE

S.M.: *(Off)* Thirty-two—go!

(Lights up: Bare stage.
ACTOR 1 *as* JEFF *enters from front door with shoebox.*
He calls:)

JEFF: Hey, Joan?
Joanie?
Look what I found.

ACTRESS 1: *(Off)* I'm in here.

JEFF: I said, I found something.

ACTRESS 1: *(Off)* I'm in here.

(JEFF shakes box, opens it, finds the kitchen knife.)

I can't hear you.

JEFF: No, I didn't say anything.

ACTRESS 1: *(Off)* I can't hear you.

(The doorbell rings.)

Did you say you found something?
Did you find something?
What did you find?

JEFF: I have to get the door, okay?
Okay, Joan?
Can you hear me?

ACTRESS 1: *(Off)* I'm in here.

JEFF: Never mind, forget it.

(JEFF exits toward front door.
JOAN, *masked as* BEAST, *quickly enters from closet, removes*
box and knife and returns to closet, closing the door again.)

(BLACKOUT)

THE THIRTY-THIRD SCENE

S.M.: *(Off)* Thirty-three—go!

(Lights up: Bare stage.)

ACTRESS 1: *(Off)* Jeff?

ACTOR 1: *(Off)* What?

ACTRESS 1: *(Off)* Can you come in here quickly please? I think I just cut myself pretty badly....

(ACTOR 1 as JEFF comes running from upstairs.)

JEFF: Yeah!
Where are you?
Joan?
Where are you?

(JEFF exits toward kitchen.)

(Off) Joanie?...

(BLACKOUT)

THE THIRTY-FOURTH SCENE

S.M.: *(Off)* Thirty-four—go!

(Lights up: Bare stage.
ACTOR 1 as JEFF enters from front door with shoebox. He calls:)

JEFF: Joan?
I found another one....

(JEFF opens box, finds chicken inside.)

There's like a chicken—a dead chicken inside here....

(JOAN, masked as BEAST, holding kitchen knife upraised, enters from closet and advances silently on JEFF.)

Here, look at this, this chicken was....

Joan?...

What are you doing, Joan?
Jesus, put that knife down!
JOANNNNNNNN!!!!

(BLACKOUT)

THE THIRTY-SIXTH SCENE

S.M.: *(Off)* Thirty-six—go!

(Lights up: ACTOR *&* ACTRESS 1 *as two* GHOSTS *are watching TV.)*

ACTRESS 1: Is there anything else on?

ACTOR 1: I don't know.
Where's the *TV Guide*?

ACTRESS 1: I don't know.

ACTOR 1: Last time I saw it was on the TV.
But it's not there now.

ACTRESS 1: No.
Besides, that was last week's.

ACTOR 1: Oh, was that last week's?

ACTRESS 1: Unh-hunh.

ACTOR 1: Then I guess I haven't seen this week's, I don't
   think.

ACTRESS 1: Well, it was on the TV the last time I saw it.
But it's not there now.

ACTOR 1: Nope.

ACTRESS 1: I don't know where it is.
Maybe we threw it out.

ACTOR 1: Could be.

ACTRESS 1: Well, that's okay.

ACTOR 1: Yep.
That's life.
I threw some stuff out but I'm not looking through the
    trash.

ACTRESS 1: No—no, no, no.

ACTOR 1: But we can change the channels, see what's
    on....
If you want.

ACTRESS 1: No, actually, this is fine.

ACTOR 1: Is this fine with you?

ACTRESS 1: Yeah, this is fine.

ACTOR 1: Yeah, actually, this is fine with me too.

ACTRESS 1: Okay.
Fine.

(BLACKOUT)

THE THIRTY-SEVENTH SCENE

S.M.: *(Off)* Thirty-seven—go!

(Lights up: ACTOR *&* ACTRESS 2 *as* BEAST *&* WITCH *are
calling:)*

WITCH: W-o-o-o-o-o-o-o-o-o-o-o-o-o-o-o-o....

BEAST: I smell the Mommy,
And I smell the Daddy,
And I smell the blood of the baby boy:
Be they near or be they far,
I'll hunt them down and eat them all!

WITCH: Come here, little children, come out from where
    you're hiding!

We know you're in here somewhere, and we have a
   surprise....

BEAST: HEY!....

HEY!....

WE'RE HERE....

(THE BEAST & WITCH *begin to talk more normally.*)

WITCH: (I don't think they're even home.)

BEAST: (Well, they didn't go far if they left the TV set
   on.)

Boy, I am really starving....

WITCH: I just hope they didn't forget.

BEAST: They'll be back, don't worry about it.

Hey, come here.

WITCH: What?

BEAST: Let's play a trick on them when they get back.
Come here, I'll show you....

(*They cross to closet, exit within and hide.*)

(*BLACKOUT*)

THE THIRTY-EIGHTH SCENE

S.M.: (*Off*) Thirty-eight—go!

(*Lights up: Bare stage.
Beat.*)

S.M.: (*Off*) And house up....

(*Houselights fade up.*)

INTERMISSION

S.M.: *(Off)* Fade house to half....
And house out....

(Houselights fade out.
Offstage, sound of the birdcall.)

S.M.: *(Off)* And blackout!

(BLACKOUT)

THE SIXTY-SEVENTH SCENE

S.M.: *(Off)* Sixty-seven—go!

(Lights up: ACTOR *&* ACTRESS 2 *as* JEFF *&* JOAN *are watching TV.)*

JEFF: Hey, Joan?

JOAN: What?

JEFF: Do we have any kandy korn?

JOAN: I can't hear you.

JEFF: Do we have any kandy korn?

JOAN: What?

JEFF: Can you hear me?

JOAN: I'm in the kitchen.

JEFF: What?

JOAN: What?

JEFF: What?

JOAN: I'm in the kitchen.

JEFF: Can you hear me?

JOAN: I can't hear you.

JEFF: Can you hear me?

JOAN: I can't hear you.

JEFF: Hey, Joan?

JOAN: I can't hear you.

JEFF: Do we have any kandy korn?

JOAN: What?

JEFF: I'm in the kitchen.

JOAN: I'm in the kitchen.

JEFF: I'm in the kitchen.

JOAN: What?

JEFF: Hey, Joan?

JOAN: What?

JEFF: Hey, Joan?

JOAN: I can't hear you.

JEFF: What?

JOAN: Hey, Joan?

JEFF: Do we have any kandy korn?

BOTH: I'm in the cupboard over the sink.

(BLACKOUT)

THE TWENTY-SIXTH SCENE

S.M.: *(Off)* Twenty-six—go!

(Lights up: ACTOR *&* ACTRESS 1 *as* JEFF *&* JOAN *are watching TV.)*

JEFF: I'm sorry I yelled at you about the door.

JOAN: That's okay.
I yelled at you too.

JEFF: No, it's my fault and I'm sorry.

JOAN: It's not all your fault.

JEFF: Well, I think it is.

But I'm not mad at you any more.

JOAN: No, I'm not mad at you either.
It's just...when you yell at me....

JEFF: I know, I know, I'm sorry....
I don't know why I get so angry sometimes.

JOAN: Well, it's partly my fault too for not....

JEFF: No, it's not your fault.
It's not.

Okay?

JOAN: Okay.

JEFF: Okay.
The end.

(Beat.
JOAN *rises, crosses to* JEFF, *kisses him.)*

(BLACKOUT)

THE TWENTY-NINTH SCENE

S.M.: *(Off)* Twenty-nine—go!

(Lights up: ACTRESS 1 *as* JOAN *is watching TV.*
THE BEAST *enters from upstairs, carrying shoebox.)*

JOAN: Oh, wow!
Is that your costume? That's great!
You really look scary.

(Actually, you don't, you look like my sweetie, but
   that's 'cause I know....)

(THE BEAST *hands* JOAN *the shoebox.*)

What?
What's this?
What is this?
Come on, tell me!
What's in here?
Jeff—how come you won't tell me?
Is there something ooky in here?
There is, isn't there?
What?
Tell me!
I'm not opening it. (I'll bet there's something gross.)
Why won't you tell me, hunh?

(THE BEAST *turns and exits toward kitchen.*)

What's wrong?
Sweetie?...
I was only kidding....
Jeff?...

(JOAN *exits after* THE BEAST, *carrying box, as*
ACTOR 1 *as* JEFF *enters from closet.*)

JEFF: Yo?...

(JEFF *sits and watches TV.*
ACTRESS 1 *screams from offstage.*)

(*Calls*) Anything wrong, sweetie?...

(*BLACKOUT*)

THE FORTY-FIFTH SCENE

S.M.: *(Off)* Forty-five—go!

(Lights up: ACTOR 1 *as* JEFF *is watching TV.*
ACTOR 2 *as* THE BEAST *enters from closet.)*

BEAST: Pssssssst!
Hey, buddy.
Hey, Jeff. (See, I know you.)
Look at this....

*(*BEAST *holds a strange, hunched-over pose in which he seems
to be pointing to something very small for a beat; then:)*

Right now! And look at this....

(Another similar pose held for a beat:)

Right now! And look at this....

(Another similar pose held for a beat:)

Right now! And look at this....

(Another similar pose held for a beat:)

Right now!
And look at you! (Right now!)
And look at me! (Right now!)
And look at everything! (Right now!)

(Runs to chair, pulls shoebox from underneath chair)

And look at this!
What is this?
What is it?
What's inside of it?
Something's inside of it.
But what?
Wouldn't you like to know?

Wouldn't you like a peek?
Wouldn't you like to find out?...

Well, too bad—you're not going to....

(And BEAST *runs off to closet carrying box.*)

(BLACKOUT)

THE FIFTY-FIRST SCENE

S.M.: (*Off*) Fifty-one—go!

(*Lights up:* ACTOR & ACTRESS 1 *as* JEFF & JOAN *are watching TV.*)

JEFF: Hey, whatever happened to that box?

JOAN: Hunh?

JEFF: The shoebox—you know....

(JEFF *points to the place where* GHOST *puts shoebox in Scene 41.*)

The white shoebox or whatever it was....
Sitting over there, it's been sitting over there.
I've been staring at the damn thing all night long.
It was yours, right?

I mean, you must have been the one to take it.

JOAN: I don't know what in God's name you're talking about.

JEFF: Hey, I'm not pissed off at you or anything.

JOAN: You're saying you saw one of my shoeboxes over there all night?

JEFF: Is this a put-on?

JOAN: Boy, you've been acting so weird....

(BLACKOUT)

THE FORTY-FIRST SCENE

S.M.: *(Off)* Forty-one—go!

(Lights up: Bare stage, birdcall sound.
A GHOST *enters stealthily from closet with shoebox.*
GHOST *places box in a fairly conspicuous place,*
exits through closet.)

(BLACKOUT)

THE FIFTY-FOURTH SCENE

S.M.: *(Off)* Fifty-four—go!

(Lights up: ACTOR 1 *as* JEFF *is watching TV. He does not*
react to ACTRESS 2 *as* JOAN, *standing in closet doorway.)*

JEFF: *(Calls)* Are you ready?...

ACTRESS 2: *(Softly)* I'm ready....

(Beat)

JEFF: *(Calls)* Joan?...
Are you ready?...

ACTRESS 2: *(Softly)* I was....

*(*ACTRESS 2 *turns and exits into closet, closing door.)*

JEFF: *(Calls)* Joan?...

...(Oh, shit....)

*(*JEFF *puts his head in his hands.)*

ACTRESS 1: *(Off)* I'm coming as fast as I can!...

(BLACKOUT)

THE FORTY-FOURTH SCENE

S.M.: *(Off)* Forty-four—go!

(Lights up: ACTOR 1 *as* JEFF *is watching TV.
Closet door opens,* BEAST *peeps out.)*

BEAST: *(Softly)* I'm in here.

*(*BEAST *pops back in, shutting door;* JEFF *doesn't react.)*

ACTRESS 1: *(Off)* What?

(Closet door opens, BEAST *peeps out.)*

BEAST: *(Softly)* I'm in here.

*(*BEAST *pops back in, shutting door;* JEFF *doesn't react.)*

ACTRESS 1: *(Off)* What?

(Closet door opens, BEAST *peeps out.)*

BEAST: *(Softly)* I'm in here.

*(*BEAST *pops back in, shutting door;* JEFF *doesn't react.*
ACTRESS 1 *as* JOAN *enters, carrying overcoats.)*

JOAN: Did you say something?

JEFF: No.
Why?

JOAN: Oh, for some reason I thought you were calling
    me.
I thought I'd just hang up our coats and neat up a little.

*(*JOAN *goes to closet and hangs up coats.)*

JEFF: Oh, yeah, never know when one of our many
    friends is going to drop by unannounced....
Certainly wouldn't want to create a bad impression by
    having a messy house.

JOAN: I know, but even so, there's no reason not to hang
   our coats up every once in a while.
After all, it's so often we neat up....

(Something reaches out and pulls JOAN *into closet.*
She screams. JEFF *doesn't react.*
Beat.)

*(*JEFF *rises and closes closet door.)*

(BLACKOUT)

THE FORTIETH SCENE

S.M.: *(Off)* Forty—go!

(Lights up: Bare stage, birdcall sounds.
ACTOR 1, *as* JEFF, *carrying the knife, enters from kitchen and*
sneaks up on closet door. The birdcall stops. JEFF *flings the*
closet door open and exits inside. ACTRESS 2, *as* WITCH,
pops in from the nearest entrance and slams closet shut.)

ACTOR 1: *(Off)* Joan?
Hey!
Let me out!
Let me out of here!
Help! Let me out!
HELLLLLLLLLLLLLLP!

(Loud banging from inside closet; WITCH *cackles.)*

(BLACKOUT)

THE SIXTY-THIRD SCENE

S.M.: *(Off)* Sixty-three—go!

(Lights up: ACTRESS 1 *as* JOAN *is watching TV.*
   two GHOSTS *stand behind her.*
ACTOR 1 *calls from offstage:)*

ACTOR 1: *(Off)* You know I love you, baby....

You know there could never be anyone like you in my
   life, don't you baby?

(The GHOSTS *slowly shroud* JOAN *with another sheet.)*

You're so magnificent.
You're so special to me.
We have something nobody else in the world has.
Let's not ruin it by being possessive.
I feel so close to you and I love to make love to you.
I just want to show you what you mean to me....
I just want to love you....
I love you....

*(*ACTOR 1*'s voice turns into animal noises; pounding from
closet.)*

(BLACKOUT)

THE FORTY-THIRD SCENE

S.M.: *(Off)* Forty-three—go!

(Lights up: A GHOST *is watching TV.*
ACTOR 1 *as* JEFF *enters from kitchen, stands against upstage
wall.)*

JEFF: Why won't you answer me?...

Why won't you talk to me?...

This is wrong, this is wrong, this is stupid and wrong!

*(*GHOST *rises and slowly walks upstairs.)*

(Calling after) I happen to love you, I'm sorry....

*(*JEFF *sits in the chair but doesn't watch TV.)*

(BLACKOUT)

THE FORTY-SEVENTH SCENE

S.M.: *(Off)* Forty-seven—go!

(Lights up: ACTOR 1 *as* JEFF *is watching TV.*
Beat.
ACTRESS 2 *as* JOAN *bursts out of closet, screaming in rage:)*

ACTRESS 2: I wish I had a dick like a man!
I wish I had that fat thing!
I wish I had something that works!
Because I have nothing!
I have nothing!
So how do you like that?
Why don't you put that in your next play?

(ACTRESS 2 *exits into closet, slamming door.)*

(BLACKOUT)

THE FORTY-SIXTH SCENE

ACTOR & ACTRESS 2: *(Off)* Forty-six—go!

(Lights up: ACTOR 1 *as* JEFF *is watching TV.*
ACTOR & ACTRESS 2 *as* BEAST & WITCH *are upstage.)*

BEAST: Do you notice anything?
Do you notice anything different?
Do you notice anything different about her?

WITCH: Don't you notice anything different about me?
Don't you notice anything about me?
Don't you notice anything?...

BEAST: Speak up, there....

WITCH: I pray you, Sir, I prithee tell,
Whether my face doth please thee well?

JEFF: Alas, the eyes deceive, I cannot tell.

WITCH: Then I pray you, Sir, I prithee tell,
Whether my voice doth please thee?

JEFF: Also, the ears deceive, as know thee well.

WITCH: Then I pray you, Sir, I prithee tell,
Whether my kiss doth please?

JEFF: The lips also deceive....

WITCH: Methinks sometimes in truth he loveth me not.

BEAST: Not so, not so, he shall protest:
There is one part of you above all others he desires,
And which he dare not name,
And that is the part above all others he desires to touch,
And yet he dare not.

WITCH: Why then, indeed, he loveth me not.

JEFF: Not so, I do protest, not so.

WITCH: Then I shall ask and you shall answer:
I pray you prithee tell
How pleaseth thee my love?

JEFF: Alas, I cannot tell, the heart deceiveth.

WITCH: Then if thou can but say thou cannot tell,
Methinks thou knowest me not,
And knowing me not, thou lovest me not,
And loving me not, thou pleaseth me not,
And so, farewell!

(BEAST & WITCH *exit into closet.*)

JEFF: Not so, good maid, I know thee well,
For thou art the Devil and I am in Hell.

(BLACKOUT)

THE FORTY-EIGHTH SCENE

S.M.: (*Off*) Forty-eight—go!

(*Lights up:* ACTOR 1 *as* JEFF *is standing downstage center. He is holding the chicken carcass by each wingtip so that the legs hang down and the body position is that of a living bird. The scene is done as a monologue directly to the audience.*

THE ACTOR *makes chicken noises and flaps the wings. He talks in a funny voice.*)

ACTOR 1: "Here I am, just a happy chicken, walking around....
And look—here come the nice people that always feed me!
Now, that's funny, the nice people have a knife....
Oh, oh—I think the people are coming to cut off my head!
Oh, no! The people want to cut off my head!
Help! Help! No—get away!
Help! I can't fly! They clipped my wings!
Oh, no! I can't run! I can't get away!
Oh, no! Here it comes!
AHHHHHHHHHHHHHHHHHHHHHH!...

(*He drops one wingtip and shakes the chicken violently.*)

Er-laddle-laddle-laddle-laddle-laddle-laddle-laddle....

Er-laddle-laddle-laddle-laddle-laddle-laddle-laddle....

YAH!

(*With a great shout he throws chicken into a corner.*)

Get away!
Get away from me!

(*He crosses to a chair, sits in front of TV.*)

Get away, dead thing.
It's a dead thing!
It's all dead, it's all pink inside and juicy....
It's all like, soft....

Somebody's going to have to eat it, you know.
Otherwise, you're not supposed to cut off the head.

Somebody better eat it....

But not me, boy, not me. I'm watching TV.

(Beat. Then suddenly he jumps up and points to the chicken.)

Get away! Get away from me!
It's all moving around, everything's all moving inside.

But you know what's really gross?
(You're supposed to say: No, what's really gross?)
What's really gross is....*(He mumbles into a cupped hand.)*

EWWWWWWWW! PRETTY GROSS, HUNH?

(And he runs upstairs.)

(BLACKOUT)

THE FORTY-NINTH SCENE

S.M.: *(Off)* Forty-nine—go!

(Lights up: ACTRESSES 1 & 2 *as* WITCHES *watch TV
throughout scene.*
ACTOR 1 *as* JEFF *is holding chicken.)*

JEFF: This is yours, isn't it? Isn't it?
Isn't it yours?
It is, isn't it?

I'm going to put it somewhere. Why don't I?
Why don't I put it somewhere for you?
Why don't I just put it somewhere?

(He puts the chicken somewhere.)

How's that?
Or...I could put it over here....

(He puts it somewhere else.)

Or...I could put it over there. (Why don't I?)

(He puts it somewhere else. These changes need not be very great.)

Or, wait—I'll put it over here....

(He puts it somewhere else.)

Or, no—wait—I'll put it over there....

(He puts it somewhere else.)

Or, maybe—no, wait—I'll put it right over here, like this.

(He puts it somewhere else.)

Or maybe like this?
You like it like this?

(He puts it somewhere else.)

Or maybe I'll just move it like this, I'll just move it
   around like this over here and like that over there I'll
   just move it all over like this and like that and just
move
   it around I'll just move it a little and just a bit more
over
   just a bit more over just a bit more over just a bit more
   over....

(BLACKOUT)

THE FIFTY-SIXTH SCENE

S.M.: *(Off)* Fifty-six—go!

(Lights up: ACTOR 1 *as* JEFF *is yelling at a* GHOST.*)*

JEFF: Get out!
Get away from here!
Get out of here!
Get away from here!
Get out!
Get out!
Get away!
Go away!
Get out!
Get ouuuuuuuuuut!
OUUUUUUUUUUUUUT!

(JEFF *becomes increasingly agitated.*
THE GHOST *never moves.*
The scene is cut short by:)

(BLACKOUT)

THE FIFTIETH SCENE

S.M.: *(Off)* Fifty—go!

(Lights up: A GHOST *sits watching TV.*
ACTOR 1, *as* JEFF, *stands against the upstage wall.)*

JEFF: There was so much...
So many things I wanted to tell you....
And I never could, the words came out all wrong,
They meant different things to you and me....
I couldn't express myself:
I'd try to explain something and every time it seemed
    the words became distorted in travelling the space
    between us.
How was it possible that we could become such
    strangers,
When we had started with an understanding that went
    beyond all words,
In which our two blind souls communicated perfectly
    by touch?

I've never known such helpless sadness.
Were we really so completely wrong about each other?
I watched you turn away from me, give up on me,
As everything became corrupted by suspicion,
And when I tried to show you how I loved you with
    such passion,
You thought it was only the sex I was after.
And you were right—that was the passion—
But you were wrong to think it wasn't love.

And in your eyes, I was just some guy out for a little
    pie....

Because you were stupid!
Stupid and square and repressed and self-righteous and
    fucked up in the head with every god-damned shitty
    little fear....
And you said you were going to free yourself?
You said you wanted everything from life?
You said you were going to take it all and grow and
    become this great artist?
How? When everything had to be so safe? Without
    risk? Without danger?
And you thought I was really going to leave this
    woman I have lived with for nine years and who has
    supported me and cared for me and loved with me
    and laughed with me and grown with me and
    suffered through this and a hundred other kinds of
    bullshit and still loves me?
Whom I will always love?
She is my other self!
And I was to leave her for you? You must be joking!
No, you were right. I was exploiting you.
Because I knew all along you were nothing and I just
    kept turning a blind eye to that because the sex was
    good.
I had no respect for you—I just used you.
And you could see that, and so eventually you rejected

me.
Except I did love you. And I still do. I still do.
Except I don't.
Except I do, don't, do, don't, do, don't....

(JEFF *takes sheet off* GHOST, *revealing* ACTRESS 1 *as* JOAN.)

Hello, Joan....

(*BLACKOUT*)

THE FIFTY-SEVENTH SCENE

(ACTOR 1 *screams.*
ACTOR 1 *screams again.*)

ACTOR 1: Help me!

(*Lights up:* ACTOR 1 *as* JEFF *is lying on the floor and screaming.*)

Help me!
Somebody help me!
Somebody please help me!
Help me, help me, help me!...
Oh, God, help me, help me, help me!...
OH—SOME-BO-DY—PLEEEEEEEEEESE HELP ME!...
(*etc.*)

(*Meanwhile the voices of the other actors are heard offstage, chanting softly. See Notes on page 87.*)

OTHERS: The demon in me
Is the demon in me!
The demon in me
Is the demon in me!
The demon in me
Is the demon in me!
The demon in me
Is the demon in me!...(*etc.*)

(JEFF's *cries become weaker as the chanting grows louder.*
Three GHOSTS *appear, each at a different entrance.)*

(BLACKOUT)

THE SIXTY-SECOND SCENE

S.M.: *(Off)* Sixty-two—go!

(Lights up: ACTRESS 1, *as* JOAN, *is watching TV.*
ACTOR 1, *as* JEFF, *appears outside window, rapping on glass.)*

JEFF: *(Calls)* Joan!...
It's me!...
Let me in!...
Help me!...
Joan, can't you see me?...
Can't you hear me?...
Help!...
Joan!...
I'm....

(GHOSTS *pull* JEFF *away.*
JOAN *never reacts.)*

AAAAAAAAAAAAAAAAAAAAAAAAAAAH!
I'm going!...
Hellllllp!...

(JEFF *disappears.*
Beat.)

(BLACKOUT)

THE SIXTY-FOURTH SCENE

S.M.: *(Off)* Sixty-four—go!

(Lights up: ACTRESS 1, *as* JOAN, *is watching TV.*
There is a sudden crashing sound offstage.)

JOAN: Jeff?...

Is that you?...

Hello?...

(Sound of someone coming down the stairs.
JOAN *rises in alarm.)*

Hello?
Who's there?
Jeff?
Who is it?...

(THE BEAST *appears with the knife in his hand and advances
on* JOAN. *She screams and tries to run away, but trips and
falls out of sightlines (e.g.: behind chair).* BEAST *then falls
upon her and stabs her to death. The effect should be as
bloody and realistic as possible. Alternatively,* JOAN *could
try and barricade herself in the closet and be stabbed there.
After the murder,* THE BEAST *exits, and there is a beat.
Then:)*

ACTOR 1: *(Off)* Joan?
Can you come here a minute?
I think I just cut myself. *(BLACKOUT)*

THE FIFTY-SECOND SCENE

S.M.: *(Off)* Fifty-two—go!

*(Lights do not come up; only TV illuminates scene.
A* BEAST *appears in the entrance to front door, moving back
and forth in a jerky, spasmodic way. See Notes on page 87.)*

BEAST: Zip....
Zip zip....
Zip....
Zip zip....

(A SECOND BEAST *begins walking in a jerky, spasmodic way
out of the closet and back, also muttering:)*

BEAST 2: Zip zip zip....
Zip zip....
Zip zip zip....
Zip zip....

(Eventually, both BEASTS *move further into the room with their odd twitching and bending movements.* ONE *begins the following chant to the rhythm established by the other. Then both join in, in unison. See Notes on page 87.)*

BEASTS: Behold the Lightning Man the Lightning
   Lightning Man
Behold the Power Power of the Power Power
Of the Lightning Man the Lightning Lightning Man
Of Power Power of the Power Power
Of the zip zip zip zip zip zip
Zip zip zip zip zip zip
Power Power zip zip
Power Power zip zip
Lightning Man the Lightning Lightning Man
BEHOLD The Lightning Man The Lightning Lightning
   Man
Behold the Power Power of the Power Power
See the Lightning Lightning
See the Lightning Lightning
Lightning Man the Power Power
Lightning Power Power
Lightning Man the zip zip
Lightning zip zip zip zip
Power zip zip Power
Power zip zip Power
Power zip zip zip zip
Zip zip zip zip zip zip
Zip zip zip zip zip zip
YAH!!!!!

*(*BEASTS *freeze on shout.*
BEASTS *exit severally.)*

(END OF SCENE)

THE SIXTY-FIFTH SCENE

(Lights do not come up; only TV illuminates the scene.
Birdcall sounds; closet door opens slowly.
A bright light from within falls across the stage.
A BEAST *stands in threshold with a shoebox held out before it.*
As THE BEAST *crosses the stage, another identical* BEAST
appears in doorway, so that a never-ending procession is set
up.
ACTRESS 2 *speaks from offstage.)*

ACTRESS 2: *(Off)* If I speak to you now
Of the primitive days
When the creatures before you
Came down to the river
To drink by the moonlight
In numberless numbers,
Will you walk on this earth
In the sunlight
Aware
Of the numberless numbers
Of creatures before you
That walked on this earth
In numberless numbers
In sunlight and perished
In layer on layer
Of earth that was walked on
By creatures that perished
In layer on layer
In numberless numbers
Alone and screaming
As you must do
As they have done?

Life feeds upon living.
We are all one eating each other.
And the primitive days are coming again.

(The door closes slowly. The last BEAST *out—it should be* ACTOR 2—*stops midstage.)*

(END OF SCENE)

THE THIRTY-NINTH SCENE

S.M.: *(Off)* Thirty-nine—go!

(A light goes on at the head of the stairs; otherwise, this scene is played by the light of the television.
ACTOR 2 *as* THE BEAST *is watching TV.* ACTRESS 2 *as* THE WITCH *enters from upstairs. She speaks in falsetto:)*

WITCH: Who's come creeping 'round my little house tonight?
Is there someone at the door? Is he coming inside?
Is it somebody who's lost and he's not where he's supposed to be?
Who can it be? Tell me who can it be?

BEAST: It's the wind, little mother, just the cold north wind
Come blowing 'round your warm little house.

WITCH: No, but somebody's eaten all the food in my cupboard,
And it can't be the wind because the wind is never hungry.
And somebody's been walking 'round all up and down and everywhere.
Who can it be? Oh, who can it be?

BEAST: It's a bird, little mother, just a frightened little bird
Seeking shelter from the stormy winds outside.

WITCH: Oh, I think somebody's lying in my little house tonight,
And it can't be a bird because a bird can't talk.

So it must be a man, and a small one by the sound of
  him.
Now who can it be? Oh, I wonder who it is?

BEAST: My name is Jack and I've come here to kill you,
And live in your cottage and eat all your food.

WITCH: Such a proud boast from such a little man!

BEAST: I have a knife!

WITCH: But the blade is too short.

BEAST: I have another knife, my father's knife.

WITCH: But see, the blade is grown so dull.

BEAST: Then kill you I shall with my own bare hands!

WITCH: But they are both so weak and I am powerful:
For you are in my house and far from home,
And you have eaten of enchanted food,
And all of this can disappear at my displeasure,
And then you would be lost again and hungry in the
  night
And alone in the heart of the cold and pitiless forest.

BEAST: But I have left a trail.

WITCH: Of crumbs, and birds have eaten them.

BEAST: But I have left another trail.

WITCH: Of stones, and the wind has covered them.
Therefore, here shall you stay,
And we in loving lay,
Forever and a day,
And I shall have my way,
Or else I will abandon you!

(THE WITCH *cackles, exits toward kitchen.*)

(*BLACKOUT*)

THE SIXTY-SIXTH SCENE

(Lights up: ACTOR *&* ACTRESS 2 *as* JEFF *&* JOAN *are watching TV.*
ACTOR 1 *speaks from offstage.*
Periodically, a GHOST *seems to pass across the window, then across the hallway to door. This should be done by using two different* GHOSTS. *The length of time between the* GHOST *disappearing from window and appearing in hall should fluctuate.)*

ACTOR 1: *(Off)* And I became spirit,
When I knew that I was spirit,
And I became spirit,
When I noticed I was spirit,
And that what I was was noticing,
And that noticing was spirit.
And I became spirit
When I noticed I was thinking
And that what I was noticing was thinking,
And that what I was was noticing and thinking,
And that noticing and thinking were spirit.
And I became spirit when I heard my name called,
And I knew it was my name,
And that the spirit called me,
And that my name was spirit.

That spirit is spirit
That walks as spirit,
In a world of spirit,
Of light and darkness,
Of inside and outside,
Of one and the other,
And all the same....

For spirit is ever there,
And nothing changes,

And everything changes,
And nothing changes,
And everything changes,
And everything changes,
And nothing changes,
And nothing changes,
And everything changes....

(BLACKOUT)

THE FIFTY-EIGHTH SCENE

S.M.: *(Off)* Fifty-eight—go!

(Lights up: ACTRESS 1, *as* JOAN, *is watching TV.*
ACTOR 1 *makes animal wails offstage, then enters as* BEAST,
holding up kitchen knife and wailing, stopping by JOAN.
Beat.)

JOAN: Stop it.

*(*ACTOR 1 *will use funny voice throughout scene.)*

BEAST: Stop what?

JOAN: You know.

BEAST: No, I don't. Stop what?

JOAN: Stop being weird. I don't like it.

BEAST: Am I being weird? I'm not being weird.
Am I being weird? I'm not being weird.
I don't know what you mean, Joan.
I'm not being weird at all.
Here, I'll show you. (I'll just put this little knife away....)

*(*BEAST *sits down.)*

See, I'm just sitting here in this very normal way
In this very normal chair in this very normal room
Looking at this very normal television program,
Just being very normal....

Right?
I mean, I think you're the one who's acting kind of
    weird, Joan.
In fact, I think you're being very very very weird
    indeed.

JOAN: Oh, shut up!
God, I think you're being stupid!
I really hate it when you get this way!

BEAST: Trick or treat!

JOAN: Fuck you!

(JOAN *storms out of the room.*)

BEAST: (Fuck you too, you rancid sack of horseshit....)

(*BLACKOUT*)

THE FORTY-SECOND SCENE

S.M.: (*Off*) Forty-two—go!

(*Lights up:* ACTRESS 1 *as* JOAN *is watching TV.
The shoebox is still where it was placed in Scene 51.*
ACTOR 1, *as* JEFF, *enters, notices box.*)

JEFF: What's this?

JOAN: What's what?

(JEFF *picks up box.*)

JEFF: This.

JOAN: I don't know.

JEFF: It's not yours?

JOAN: No.

JEFF: Hunh. Weird.

JOAN: Why? It's not yours?

JEFF: No. It was just sitting right here.

JOAN: That's weird.
What's inside it?

JEFF: I don't know.
This twine is that plastic stuff that's impossible to cut.

JOAN: You want a knife?
I'll get you a knife.
They're pretty dull, but....

JEFF: Yeah, maybe I better....

JOAN: Okay.

(JOAN *exits toward kitchen.*
While she is gone, JEFF *manages to slide off string.*
He opens the box and lets out a cry of fear and disgust,
quickly closes box and puts it down, and stands away,
wiping his hands as JOAN *runs in from kitchen.)*

JOAN: What is it?

JEFF: Don't come in here!

JOAN: What?

JEFF: Just get me a plastic trashbag.
Do we have any plastic trashbags?
Quick!

JOAN: All right!

(JOAN *exits toward kitchen.)*

JEFF: Have you got one?

JOAN: *(Off)* In a minute.... All right, I've got one.

JEFF: Just stay where you are.
I want you to hold the bag open at the top and I'm
   going to bring this thing in there....

(*Gingerly picking up box,* JEFF *walks quickly into kitchen.)*

(*Off*) Keep the bag away from your body, out from your
   body....

ACTOR 2: (*From closet*) Let...meeee...ouuuuuuuuut....

(*BLACKOUT*)

THE FIFTY-FIFTH SCENE

S.M.: (*Off*) Fifty-five—go!

(*Lights up:* ACTOR 1, *as* JEFF, *stands by the window.*
ACTRESS 2 *is visible outside, smiling.*)

JEFF: When will I see you again?
I would give anything to see you again.
I keep thinking of you all the time, at every hour,
Alone and in the company of others.
I keep on seeing your resemblance in the faces of others.
I keep you hidden in my secret thoughts and close to
   me.
I keep on thinking that I'll see you once again somehow,
I keep on saying so, but I don't believe it:
Never as you were then,
Alive and real in front of me
In a room with a door and a bed and a lock,
Because even then, no matter how I tried to hold you,
I could not keep you....

(*The doorbell rings.*)

I couldn't keep you....

(ACTRESS 2 *disappears by walking backwards as doorbell
rings again.*)

And I despair of seeing you again....

(ACTRESS 1 *as* JOAN *enters from upstairs.*)

I know—don't worry—I'll get the door.

JOAN: I wasn't thinking about that.
It's way too late and we're all out of candy.
Fuck 'em—we're not home.

(JOAN *hugs* JEFF.)

You about ready to go to bed?

JEFF: Oh, I can't sleep.
I'm going to have at least another drink,
Watch some more TV—I don't know....

JOAN: Well, let me get it for you.

You don't mind, do you?

JEFF: I don't mind.

(JOAN *is exiting toward kitchen.*)

I love you.

(JOAN *returns, touches his face, kisses him.*)

JOAN: I love you too.

(JOAN *exits toward kitchen.*)

(*BLACKOUT*)

THE SIXTY-FIRST SCENE

S.M.: (*Off*) Sixty-one—go!

(*Lights up:* ACTRESS 1 *as* JOAN *is watching TV.*
ACTOR *&* ACTRESS 2 *call offstage;* JOAN *does not react.*)

ACTOR 2: (*Off*) Joan? We're going....

ACTRESS 2: (*Off*) We're going, Joan....

ACTOR 2: (*Off*) Come on, Joan, we're going....

ACTRESS 2: (*Off*) Come on, Joan....

ACTOR 2: (*Off*) We're going....

ACTRESS 2: *(Off)* Hurry, Joanie, hurry....

ACTOR 2: *(Off)* Come on, we're going....

ACTRESS 2: *(Off)* Joanie!...

ACTOR 2: *(Off)* Hurry, Joanie, hurry....

ACTRESS 2: *(Off)* Come on, Joan....

ACTOR 2: *(Off)* Here we go, Joan!....

ACTRESS 2: *(Off)* Goodbye!...

ACTOR 2: *(Off)* Goodbye! We're going!...

ACTRESS 2: *(Off)* Goodbye, Joan!...

(Silence.

JOAN *rises, changes TV channels, sits again.)*

(BLACKOUT)

THE FIFTY-THIRD SCENE

S.M.: *(Off)* Fifty-three—go!

(Lights up: ACTOR *&* ACTRESS 1, *as* JEFF *&* JOAN, *are watching TV.* ACTOR 2 *appears from kitchen as* BEAST.*)*

ACTOR 2: Hey, you guys?
We were just thinking of going to the DQ.
We were both thinking maybe we'd do that.
How about it? You want to go?
You want to go to the DQ?
You're welcome to come along.
But...we're going—we're—we're going to go—unh—
We're going in five maybe ten minutes.
Maybe fifteen tops she's in there taking a leak or
   something.
So—you want to go to the DQ, hunh?
You want to go?
Or maybe not.

No problem.
It's just something we thought—we kind of got into
    it—unh....
Actually it was her idea.
But you don't have to, unh....
If you want us to get you something....
You want us to get you something?

Okay—well—
We'll be—unh—we'll be out there getting ready if you,
    unh...
You know, if you want....

(ACTOR 2 *exits.* JEFF *&* JOAN *have not reacted. Beat.*
JEFF *turns to* JOAN.)

JEFF: You want to go?

JOAN: I don't know.
You want to go.

JEFF: There's nothing on....

JOAN: Okay, let's go.

(*BLACKOUT*)

THE SEVENTIETH SCENE

S.M.: (*Off*) Scene seventy—go!

(*Lights up: Bare stage; birdcall sounds.*
A GHOST *enters from closet and crosses to window.*
The GHOST *pulls down the windowshade.*
On the windowshade are these words:)

THE END

(*BLACKOUT*)

AFTERWORD

SEVENTY SCENES OF HALLOWEEN was always intended as a set of scenes to be recombined for each new production. Yet to my knowledge, since the play was first produced only one director has rearranged the order Matthew Maguire and I eventually arrived at. Ironically, though, trial and error was such an integral part of the initial production that four scenes were dropped from the order late in rehearsal. Because the publicity had already gone to the printers, we stayed with the original title, which I afterwards retained for its euphony. Methodical individuals, however, have always been troubled by the play's short weight, so to mollify them, and encourage all future directors at least to consider rearranging the text, the missing scenes are herewith included:

THE FIFTY-NINTH SCENE

S.M.: *(Off)* Fifty-nine—go!

(Lights up: ACTOR 2, as BEAST, is watching TV. ACTRESS 1, as JOAN, enters from upstairs. BEAST watches TV throughout scene.)

BEAST: Are you ready?

JOAN: What?

BEAST: Are you ready to go?
We're going.

JOAN: What about Jeff?

BEAST: Jeff's not coming.
It's just you.
He's already gone.
It's just you.

JOAN: He's gone already?

BEAST: Yeah, come on.
Let's go, Joan.

JOAN: Oh, I don't know—now I'm all confused.
I'm just all...
I don't know....

I'll tell you, when I was up in the bedroom getting
    ready,
This tremendous feeling of emptiness just came over
    me.
The whole thing just seemed so pointless all of a
    sudden.
I don't know, I guess everybody feels that way
    sometimes.

You think you know somebody, but you never really
    know people.
You get these ideas in your head,
You think that's the way things are,
But they're not.
Things just don't always behave the way you want
    them to.
I don't know.

Sometimes I feel like I just don't know anything,
And I never did know anything,
And I never will.
Not really....

I don't know.
Let's go, okay?
Or let's not, I don't care.... *(BLACKOUT)*

THE SIXTIETH SCENE

S.M.: *(Off)* Scene sixty—go!

(Lights up: ACTOR 2, *as* BEAST, *is watching TV, working birdcall.*
ACTRESS 1 *as* JOAN *enters.)*

BEAST: Joan?

JOAN: Yes?

BEAST: Do you have any?

JOAN: Yes.

BEAST: Good, that's very good.
Tell me, what do you have?

JOAN: Corn, I have corn,
I have corn, I have corn,
And corn and corn and corn and corn and corn and
corn and corn.

BEAST: Good, that's very good.
Tell me, where is the corn?

JOAN: The corn is asleep.

BEAST: And where is it sleeping?

JOAN: It is hidden in darkness.

BEAST: Good, very good, let it sleep.
Now then: Can it be touched?

JOAN: No, it cannot be touched.

BEAST: No, it can and it can't—it depends on the time.
There are times when we touch it and times when we
can't.
And what do we do with the corn when we touch it?

JOAN: We touch the corn to kill the corn.

BEAST: And what do we use in the killing of corn?

JOAN: We use the knife to kill the corn.

BEAST: And why do we kill the corn that we kill?

JOAN: We kill it to eat it; we kill it to bury it.

BEAST: And why do we eat the corn that we eat?

JOAN: We eat the corn and the corn brings us life.

BEAST: And why do we bury the corn that we bury?

JOAN: We bury the corn and bring the corn life.
And this is the nature, the nature of corn.

BEAST: As it was in the old days before you were born.
And how will it be when you're buried and gone?

JOAN: As it was in the old days before I was born.

BEAST: And nothing changes.

JOAN: And everything changes.

BEAST: And everything changes.

JOAN: And nothing changes.

BEAST: Good, that's very good.
Now, I shall rise and go,
And after a little while, you shall follow me....

(BEAST *exits by closet.*)

(*BLACKOUT*)

THE SIXTY-EIGHTH SCENE

S.M.: (*Off*) Sixty-eight—go!

(*Lights up: Bare stage.*
ACTOR & ACTRESS 1, *as* BEAST & WITCH, *enter from upstairs.*)

WITCH: It's a little hard to see, but....

BEAST: Yeah, but we don't have to stay this way forever.

WITCH: No, I know—I'll be okay, I think.

BEAST: See, and then once we've been there a little,
We can change back and be regular instead of going
    around in some dumb costume all night.

WITCH: No, I think it's a great idea.

(BEAST *has gone to closet and taken out two light coats.*)

BEAST: Will this be enough, you think?
You're not going to be cold, are you?

WITCH: It's not that cold out, is it?
It's not that cold.
Besides, we're driving.

BEAST: Yeah, no, it's not that cold.
Boy, I'd sure hate to get pulled over dressed like this,
    though.

WITCH: Really.

BEAST: I'm sure they see some really weird people.

(BEAST & WITCH *are exiting toward front door.*)

Are we going in your car?

WITCH: We can.

BEAST: Yeah, I'd really appreciate that.
I'll lock up, though.

(*By now they are off.*
ACTOR & ACTRESS 2, *as* JEFF & JOAN, *descend the stair,
hand in hand.*)

ACTRESS 1: (*Off*) Okay. You've got door keys?

ACTOR 1: (*Off*) Yeah.

ACTRESS 1: (*Off*) Great. I'll go start the car.

ACTOR 1: (*Off*) Okay.

(ACTOR & ACTRESS 2 *cross to window and look out, waving goodbye.*)

(*BLACKOUT*)

THE SIXTY-NINTH SCENE

S.M.: (*Off*) Sixty-nine—go!

(*Lights up:* ACTRESS 1, *as* JOAN, *is watching TV.*
ACTOR 1 *calls from closet:*)

ACTOR 1: (*Off*) Joan?...You out there?

JOAN: Unh-hunh....

ACTOR 1: (*Off*) Listen—uh—have I been looking okay to
 you lately?

JOAN: What?

ACTOR 1: (*Off*) I haven't been looking a little strange to
 you?

JOAN: What's the matter?
Are you worried about the way you look or....

ACTOR 1: (*Off*) DON'T COME IN HERE!

JOAN: I'm not—Jesus, I could care less.

ACTOR 1: (*Off*) What made you say that?

JOAN: What?

ACTOR 1: (*Off*) There's nothing wrong with the way I
 look, Joan.

Uh—actually, that's not really true.
Joan?
Actually, uh, Joan—you may find this kind of hard to
 believe,
But I think I've turned into this—kind of a—beast.
In fact, I know I have, that's why I'm in here.
And I—uh—I really don't want you to see me this way,

That's very important to me right now, I'm feeling kind
of vulnerable....

I suppose you're wondering what I look like.
Actually, I didn't get that long of a look in the mirror,
but
It's pretty gross, Joan, it's pretty bad.
You probably don't want to see me this way, hunh?
It's really pretty sickening, actually—you wouldn't
want to have to see me, I'm sure.

JOAN: Well, I don't know.

ACTOR 1: (*Off*) No, no, it's bad, it's really bad, it's
terrible.

JOAN: Oh, okay. If you say so.

ACTOR 1: (*Off*) Well, I mean, I could come out if you
wanted.
I mean, just one quick shot, you know.
That might not be such a bad idea—so you'd know, I
mean.
You better get ready, though.
No, I'm serious, Joan:
You might want to be over by the door or put your
hands over your eyes or something....

Just one last thing, I...
I want you to know I still love you,
And I really admire you for doing this, but
If, you know, you don't love me or something, listen—
I'll understand.

JOAN: Okay.

ACTOR 1: (*Off*) Okay.
Well, here goes.

(ACTOR 1, *as* JEFF, *enters from closet.*)

See what I mean?
Pretty disgusting, hunh?

Pretty revolting, hunh?
Makes you really want to puke, doesn't it?

Listen, you don't have to keep looking at me out of
  courtesy.
I understand.

JOAN: You look fine.

JEFF: Joan—look—you don't have to...pretend to me....

JOAN: You look perfectly normal.

JEFF: Joan....

JOAN: Why don't you come sit down and watch some
  TV?

JEFF: Okay—I think we both know what you're doing.

(JEFF *sits down.*)

If that's the way you want to deal with it—hey, that's
  fine.
No—honestly—maybe this is the best way.
And any time you want to like talk about it or....

JOAN: I'm trying to watch this program.

JEFF: Oh.
Okay.
Sure.

(*BLACKOUT*)

A NOTE ON CHANTING

The chants in Scenes 52 and 57 both call for resonant,
nasal vocalizations performed to regular beats. They are
written in iambs (units of an unstressed syllable
followed by a stressed syllable), and I have tried to
indicate the rhythms below by using asterisks (*) over
the stressed syllables.

      *   *   *   *   *   *
The demon in me is the demon in me! (pause)

      *   *   *   *   *   *
The demon in me is the demon in me! (pause)

      *   *   *   *   *   *
The demon in me is the demon in me! (pause)

         *   *   *   *
BEAST 1: Zip....(pause)....Zip zip....(pause)(etc)

        *   *   *   *
BEAST 2: Zip zip zip....Zip zip....(pause)(etc.)

        *   *   *   *
BEASTS: Behold the Lightning Man the Lightning
 *   *   *
Lightning Man....(pause)

   *   *   *   *   *
Behold the Power Power of the Power Power

     *   *   *   *   *
Of the Lightning Man the Lightning Lightning Man

   *   *   *   *
Of Power Power of the Power Power

       *   *   *
Of the zip zip zip zip zip zip

 *   *   *
Zip zip zip zip zip zip

 *   *   *
Power Power zip zip

  *   *   *
Power Power zip zip

 *   *   *   *   *
Lightning Man the Lightning Lightning Man

   *   *   *   *   *
BEHOLD The Lightning Man The Lightning Lightning
 *
Man

   *   *   *   *   *
Behold the Power Power of the Power Power

 *   *   *
See the Lightning Lightning

 *   *   *
See the Lightning Lightning

 *   *   *   *
Lightning Man the Power Power

 *   *   *
Lightning Power Power

 *   *   *
Lightning Man the zip zip

 *   *   *
Lightning zip zip zip zip

   *   *   *

Power zip zip Power

   *   *   *

Power zip zip Power

   *   *   *

Power zip zip zip zip

   *   *   *

Zip zip zip zip zip zip

   *   *   *

Zip zip zip zip zip zip

   *

YAH!!!!!

Lightning Source UK Ltd.
Milton Keynes UK
UKHW020928181219
355605UK00014B/1207/P